The Thriving Woman's Guide to Setting Boundaries Journal

Dear Ashlee,

Thank you for doing what you do.

Warmly,

Kim Buck

The Thriving Woman's Guide to Setting Boundaries Journal

Discover What's Stopping You From Setting Boundaries

Kim Buck, M.B.A.

The Thriving Woman's Guide to Setting Boundaries Journal:
Discover What's Stopping You From Setting Boundaries
Kim Buck, M.B.A.

Published by The Catalyst Group International Inc.
Calgary, Alberta T2W 0M2 Canada
403-255-3235

Published in Canada

ISBN: 0973993995
ISBN 13: 9780973993998

Table Of Contents

Welcome

I am delighted that you picked up this journal. It means that you desire to have a deeper understanding of your boundaries and what is stopping you from setting boundaries in your life. Understanding where we are at is the first step in changing anything. I congratulate you on your desire to gain awareness.

Essentially, *The Thriving Woman's Guide to Setting Boundaries* was written to answer the question, "Is it selfish to set boundaries?" Most of the chapters showed in different ways and through different stories that setting boundaries and having internal operating instructions for yourself and external operating instructions for all others is essential to live a healthy life. It also showed through the chapters and stories that not having boundaries is selfish because it makes it difficult for others to interact with you easily.

This guided journal is designed to bring you awareness of your thoughts, feelings, beliefs, subconscious programming and patterns around boundaries. Often we know we need to make changes in our lives, but we don't have the awareness of what's going on behind the challenges. Awareness precedes a shift and awareness precedes action. Sometimes all that we require in order to make a change is to become aware of what is truly holding us back from making this change. Often we require awareness first and then we need to change the thoughts, feelings, beliefs, subconscious programming or patterns that are the glue behind our current state of being.

Use this guided journal to bring awareness to your thoughts, feelings, beliefs, subconscious programming and patterns that are keeping you stuck. Use the Magnetic Field Release™ and The Emotion Code™ processes described in Chapter 17 in *The Thriving Woman's Guide to Setting Boundaries* to release these thoughts, feelings, beliefs, subconscious programming and patterns. Don't just become aware of what is going on for you without releasing and changing these for yourself.

Sometimes awareness will move 99% of the energy associated with a particular unsupportive thought, feeling, belief, subconscious program or pattern. Using the releasing processes will release the rest. Sometimes awareness doesn't move any energy and you need to do the releasing processes in order to release all of this stuck energy. Either way, don't just stop at awareness. You are cheating yourself if you stop there.

Setting boundaries will become possible as you release what is stopping you from doing so now and will assist you in moving easily into Woman Energy™. Once you move into Woman Energy™, the Master Boundary, setting boundaries will become much simpler and you will feel more powerful in the process.

Release all of the societal programming that tells you, as a woman, that you are supposed to take care of everything and everyone. Release the mind junk that tells you that taking care of yourself is not important. Release all of the programming that tells you to feel guilty for living your life in a way that works for you. Release the conditioning that tells you that you need to remain miserable and in a state of chaos because that is how the people around you choose to live. Release the negative thinking that says you don't have the right to make changes that will help you live in the energy of ease. Release what holds you back from having the structure in your life that will allow your energy to flow in ways that support your highest version of yourself.

Take your time as you work through this journal. Allow yourself the space to have ah-ha's. Give yourself the respect you deserve in getting to know yourself better. Be kind with yourself as you go through this journal. This process isn't about blaming yourself for all of the times you didn't have boundaries but should have. This process is about coming to a place of understanding as to why you didn't believe you had the right to set boundaries.

You deserve to discover what's stopping you from becoming Woman Energy™ and setting boundaries with ease. You deserve to become aware of why you believe you need to live your life in a way that benefits others and tramples you in the process.

Be sure to write your answers down. You will gain much greater understanding and awareness of what is going on for you if you write your answers down. Saying them out loud or to yourself won't give you as much clarity as writing them down will. There are many benefits to the process of using pen(cil) and paper.

For starters, writing forces you to focus on one thing at a time. When you are just saying the answers, you can get distracted with all kinds of mind activity and not really gain anything from the answers. When you write your answers down, the process of writing forces you to be present and attend to this one activity. When you are present, you will have much greater insights into your unsupportive thoughts, feelings, beliefs, subconscious programming and patterns than if you were busy thinking of all kinds of different things. In addition, when you actually see the words on the page you will start to see connections and interrelationships between these thoughts, feelings, beliefs, subconscious programming and patterns and the triggers that cause you to experience them over and over. If you simply say your answers out loud, you will likely miss these connections and interrelationships. If you are going to invest your time in this process and this book, you might as well receive maximum benefit from it.

Release the thoughts, feelings, beliefs, subconscious programming and patterns that stop you from setting boundaries as you become aware of them. Release them using the releasing processes mentioned earlier. Don't wait until sometime in the future to let them go. It is much easier to release these ah-ha's as you discover and uncover them than to try to remember what they are in the future.

Where I have had new insights around boundaries since I wrote *The Thriving Woman's Guide to Setting Boundaries* I have included them in this Journal. They will show up as **New Insights**.

Introduction

My Story

I shared my story with you in *The Thriving Woman's Guide to Setting Boundaries* because I wanted you to pay attention to what is going on for you. We all have different things going on. The point is for you to become aware of where your life isn't working for you. That is all that matters.

Key points of this chapter:

* Crappy, endless, exhausting, thankless work on behalf of others is killing you.
* You can't want more for someone than they want for themselves. You will only burn yourself out trying.
* When you are the dependable person who always takes care of everyone no one has to step up to do it. You give everyone an easy way out.
* You don't have to say yes to everything every time.
* You have the right to say no to everything and all things and that in doing so, you honor yourself and require others to step up.
* Just because you are expected to do something doesn't mean that you have to do something.
* Being the dependable one is a slippery slope to a disengaged life.
* Being the dependable one drains you of your life force, your dreams and any sense of sanity.
* You have the right to set boundaries and live your life in a more peaceful, engaged way.
* You are not here, on earth, to save everyone. That is not your job. That is not your responsibility.
* You deserve to live your life and not carry others through theirs.

What came up for you as you read my story?

Did my story highlight areas in your life where you really needed to have boundaries but didn't? What are these areas?

What prevented you from having boundaries in these areas?

Are you ready to set boundaries in these areas? If not, what stops you from doing this?

Are you ready to set boundaries in all areas of your life? If not, in what areas are you not yet ready to set boundaries?

Why is setting boundaries in this (these) area(s) difficult?

What was your biggest awareness or ah-ha from this chapter?

Did you release the unsupportive thoughts, feelings, beliefs, subconscious program-ming or patterns that came up for you as you worked through this chapter? If not, why not? Don't cheat yourself by skipping this step.

Section One

Understanding Boundaries and Why They Are Required

Chapter 1

What is a Boundary?

Sometimes we simply need a new definition of something for us to make use of it. When you look at something differently, what you look at changes. This changes how you feel about it and how you can successfully use it or interact with it.

Key points in this chapter:

* Boundaries are multidimensional.
* Physical boundaries are property lines, and they let everyone know what property is yours and what property is mine.
* We need a definition of boundaries that speaks to all the parts of us.
* Setting boundaries around our physical energy, mental and emotional well-being and psychological, psychic and spiritual spaces are required if we want to live a life that is fulfilling and joyful.
* We struggle to understand the consequences of not respecting someone's mental, emotional, psychological, psychic and spiritual spaces.
* We think it is selfish, greedy, unkind or not nice to have limits in place that others have to respect and not violate.
* Boundaries are operating instructions for you and everyone you interact with.
* Internal operating instructions are for ourselves and external operating instructions are for everything or everyone outside of ourselves.
* You teach people how to treat you.
* On a subconscious level, everyone is seeking to uncover your operating instructions.

* Boundaries, or the snap-back point, help people feel more at ease.
* The point in having operating instructions is to let people know how to successfully interact with you.
* Think of a boundary as your purse or handbag.
* Your purse contains everything you are responsible for.
* Your purse contains your internal operating instructions.
* Your purse contains your external operating instructions.
* Your purse contains your full responsibility for your physical well-being and your physical space; your mind and your thought processes; all of your emotions; your psychological well-being; your psychic well-being; and all of your dreams and desires and your truth.
* Setting boundaries is a requirement for healthy interactions and a healthy, fulfilled life.

Internal Operating Instructions are mentioned throughout *The Thriving Woman's Guide to Setting Boundaries*. Here is the list of these Internal Operating Instructions:

You are responsible for yourself.

You don't have to do everything by yourself. You are responsible for asking for assistance.

You say no when it doesn't serve you to say yes.

In order for others to respect you, you have to respect yourself first.

It is necessary for you to live your life in a way that pleases you, instead of living a life that pleases others and tramples you in the process.

Others get to live a life that pleases them without you demanding something from them or without you guilting them into something.

You value yourself enough to develop trust in yourself and to develop mastery.

You take care of for yourself what you would normally expect others to take care of for you.

Standing in your truth gives others permission to stand in their truth.

You see yourself as secure. You see others as competent and capable of self-sufficiency.

You respect your time, your energy, your resources and your dreams.

From the day your children are born, you see them becoming self-sufficient and having the ultimate security – being able to meet their own needs.

You encourage your children to carry their own age-appropriate purses or gym bags. You encourage them to find solutions to their problems. You don't expect them to carry your purse.

You have the power within to protect your time, your energy, your resources, your truth and your dreams. You are not counting on or demanding someone else do this for you. As well, you are not taking over someone else's life to do it for him or her.

You do not allow yourself to be taken for granted or taken advantage of.

You do not allow yourself to intrude into other people's lives. You are a full participant in your own life.

You do not fling your emotions all over the place. You do not expect others to be responsible for your feelings, especially for your happiness. You understand that you are responsible for that.

You are not self-abusive. You believe you are a woman of value and worth.

You watch the words you use. Choose and use words with higher vibrations. Stop yourself from using lower vibrating words.

You pay attention to your emotions. In any given moment, you can choose a higher vibrating emotion.

To thrive, you need to release trapped emotions and negative thoughts, feelings, beliefs, subconscious programming and patterns.

Be present and mindful.

Be grounded in your body.

Retrain your body to be in an oxytocin state and out of an adrenaline state.

Choose to step out of guilt.

Pursue your dreams and desires. You are responsible for figuring out your desires.

Do not expect your children to parent you. That isn't their job, nor is it their responsibility. It is your job as their parent to parent them, not the other way around.

Do not expect your children to be responsible for your emotions, especially for your happiness. This is your responsibility and only you can make you happy.

Do not live your life through your children. You are required, as a healthy, vibrant adult to have and pursue your own dreams and desires and you need to expect and give space to your children to have and pursue their own dreams and desires.

Do not make your children feel they aren't smart enough to figure things out on their own. They need your guidance and direction and, equally important, they need the space to work things out on their own. This is how we develop a sense of mastery.

Do not burden your children with all of your problems. Sharing all of your problems with them makes their world feel very unsafe.

Keep your physical self and your physical environment safe.

Protect your psychic space.

Protect your spiritual space.

External Operating Instructions are also mentioned throughout *The Thriving Woman's Guide to Setting Boundaries.* Here is the list:

You establish limits on what you are willing to tolerate in your life – the behaviors, requests, people, experiences, activities – and you express what these limits are.

You have limits on other people's expectations of you.

You have clearly stated expectations of how your children treat you.

You have clearly stated expectations of how your husband/partner treats you.

You have clearly stated expectations of how people outside of your immediate family treat you.

You have clearly stated expectations for your children's (under-aged or grown) behavior.

You are clear with your husband/partner on what he can do to please you.

You are clear with everyone that they are required to carry their own age-appropriate purses or gym bags.

New Insight

Whom are you betraying when it comes to setting boundaries? This is a powerful question. Are you betraying your mother for wanting to set boundaries? Are you betraying your father? Are you betraying a cultural directive that states that you must do everything others ask of you in order for you to be accepted by your group? Are you betraying the rules of your faith if you set boundaries? Do you feel trapped by this sense of betrayal? If you feel that you will be betraying someone or something if you set boundaries you will never set them. Releasing this sense of betrayal will set you free to pursue what is in your heart and live a more joyful life with ease.

Why did you pick up The Thriving Woman's Guide to Setting Boundaries? What wasn't working well in your life at that time?

Before reading The Thriving Woman's Guide to Setting Boundaries, how did you define a boundary? Allow yourself to express all of the negative meanings you had of boundaries.

How did that definition make you feel?

How do you define a boundary now?

If you have a new definition, how does it make you feel about boundaries? Does this definition make it possible for you to set boundaries now? How and why?

How easy was it for you to set boundaries in the past? If it was difficult, what made it so?

How easy is it for you to set boundaries now? What has changed for you?

If nothing has changed, are you determined to prove that it is impossible for you to set boundaries? If so, whom are you proving this to?

Do you have boundaries in some areas of your life? Identify these areas.

Do you struggle to set boundaries in the other areas of your life? Identify these areas.

Why do you struggle to set boundaries in these areas? Is there a different reason for each struggle?

What is your intention with your boundaries? What do you wish to achieve with boundaries? Do you have a different intention for boundaries in different areas of your life? If so, identify these areas and intentions.

Do you feel you are betraying someone or something if you finally set boundaries? If so, whom or what?

What are **your** internal operating instructions? Do you have any?

What internal operating instructions do you need to add for your life to be more peaceful? Are you willing to add these to your purse?

*What are **your** external operating instructions? Do you have any?*

What external operating instructions do you need to add for your life to be easier? Are you willing to add these to your purse?

What was your biggest awareness or ah-ha from this chapter?

Did you release the unsupportive thoughts, feelings, beliefs, subconscious programming or patterns that came up for you as you worked through this chapter? If not, why not? Don't cheat yourself by skipping this step.

Chapter 2

❖ ❖ ❖

Mother Energy™, Daughter Energy™ and Woman Energy™

Mother Energy™, Daughter Energy™, and Woman Energy™ describe the different archetypes that women embody. Throughout history, women have only had Mother Energy™ and Daughter Energy™ models through which they lived their lives. These archetypes were imposed on women and women were rewarded by society for fulfilling these roles. Only in the last hundred years or so have women been able to embody a new energy. This new energy is the Woman Energy™.

Key points in this chapter:

* We predominantly live our life in one of the two expected archetypes.
* Unless we are anchored in Woman Energy™, we can move in and out of the other energy as we go through the day.
* Energy is always seeking balance.
* Unless you are in Woman Energy™, different relationships, interactions, environments, expectations and experiences will require you to drop into the other energy in order to keep the energy balanced.

What was your reaction when you read this chapter in The Thriving Woman's Guide to Setting Boundaries?

Could you identify your own patterns? What jumped out at you first?

What was your biggest awareness or ah-ha from this chapter?

Did you release the unsupportive thoughts, feelings, beliefs, subconscious programming or patterns that came up for you as you worked through this chapter? If not, why not? Don't cheat yourself by skipping this step.

Chapter 3

✦ ✦ ✦

What is Mother Energy™?

Women in Mother Energy™ are the dependable, caring, doing, responsible, protective, rescuing women that we turn to in a crisis. They put everyone's needs before their own and feel selfish if they take time for themselves.

Key points in this chapter:

* Women in Mother Energy™ feel desperate to be needed.
* Mother Energy™ says, "I will take care of you because you can't take care of yourself.
* There are two sides to Mother Energy™ and both of them are unhealthy for you as a woman.
* The first side is the selfless doer. This energy is Mother Energy™ - Taken Advantage of.
* This woman is always available to take care of everyone's needs.
* Everyone can count on her to rescue them and bail them out of their crisis. This makes her feel special.
* She is an enabler. She enables others to be irresponsible for their own lives. She enables others to never experience the consequences of their actions and choices.
* She feels exhausted, numb and resentful.
* She doesn't want to offend others by saying no.
* This side of Mother Energy™ is sinister to you because you are being manipulated and taken advantage of by others. Your needs don't matter to you and they certainly don't matter to others.
* The other side of Mother Energy™ is sinister to others. This is Mother Energy™ - Intrusive.
* This side is manipulating and intrusive.

* This woman busies herself in other people's lives and not in her own.
* She believes other people are broken and need to be fixed.
* Assisting others is always with the energy that they need to do it her way.
* She believes that she knows what is best for everyone.
* She is surprised that the people around her don't know what is wrong with them.

Are you in Mother Energy™? If so, are you mainly in Mother Energy™ - Taken Advantage of? Or, are you mainly in Mother Energy™ - Intrusive?

❖   ❖   ❖

How do you demonstrate this?

Are you in Mother Energy™ - Taken Advantage of with some people and Mother Energy™ – Intrusive with others? If so, with whom are you in Mother Energy™ - Taken Advantage of? With whom are you in Mother Energy™ - Intrusive?

How do you feel when you are interacting with these people? How do you want to feel when interacting with these people?

What triggers you to move from one side of the energy to the other?

Is it your job or responsibility to take care of everyone and everything? If so, why? Are you a bad person for not doing this? If so, why?

If you are in Mother Energy™ - Taken Advantage of are you aware that you are being taken advantage of when it is happening? How do you feel when this is happening?

Do you believe people (except for young children) can take care of themselves? Properly? Do you believe people (except for young children) should take care of themselves? If so, why? If not, why not?

Will things get done if you don't do them? Is this true?

Do you receive any joy from everything you do? From what do you receive joy? What takes away your joy?

If you are mainly in Mother Energy™ - Intrusive, are you aware that you are intruding in other people's lives? Do you feel powerful when you are intrusive? How would you feel if you realized that people don't need your "assistance" as much

as you think they do? How would you feel if you had some time to yourself? Does this thought scare you?

If you are mainly in Mother Energy™ - Taken Advantage of, how would you feel if people needed you less and less? How would you feel if you required people to take care of their own age-appropriate needs? How would you feel if you had some time to yourself? Does this thought scare you?

Regardless of which side of Mother Energy™ you are in, are you worthy of having your needs met? If not, why not? Are you worthy and deserving of giving your life attention and focus? If not, why not?

What is your biggest fear if you required the people in your life (not under-aged children) to be responsible for themselves?

Are you allowing your under-aged children to try and fail and try again? If not, why not? How would you feel if you required your under-aged children to **develop** responsibility for themselves?

Are you a good mother or a bad mother if you expect your children to take care of age-appropriate responsibilities? Why? Are you harming them if you expect this?

Do you need to control everything and everyone? Be honest with yourself. If so, where does this drive to control all come from? Do you feel out of control if everything isn't done your way? If so, why? Is it possible that there are other ways of doing things besides your way? Does this thought cause you to feel stress? If so, why?

What part of your life is out of control? Be honest with yourself. You can't change what you won't acknowledge. Would you like to let go of the tight grip you have on everything and everyone? Would you be okay if you did this?

What was your biggest awareness or ah-ha from this chapter?

Did you release the unsupportive thoughts, feelings, beliefs, subconscious programming or patterns that came up for you as you worked through this chapter? If not, why not? Don't cheat yourself by skipping this step.

Chapter 4

✦ ✦ ✦

What is Daughter Energy™?

Daughter Energy™ is all about you. Daughter Energy™ is "What's in it for me? What can you do for me?" Women in Daughter Energy™ feel desperate to have their needs met. Daughter Energy™ says, "You need to take care of me because I can't do it for myself." Women in this energy have a singular focus of getting others to be responsible for them and to take care of them.

Key points in this chapter:

* There are two sides to Daughter Energy™. Daughter Energy™ - Entitled is self-absorbed, ir-responsible, selfish and manipulative.
* This woman is too consumed with her own needs to pay attention to what is going on around her.
* Daughter Energy™ - Entitled is abusive toward others. The other side of Daughter Energy™ is abusive toward the self.
* A Daughter Energy™ - Self-Abusive woman is terrified that her needs will never be met.
* She compares herself to other women and feels less attractive or less successful or less worthy or all of these.
* This woman is prone to self-abuse through various ways including eating disorders, excessive shyness or by being excessively sexual.
* She believes that no one will or can love her. She is full of fear.
* Women in Daughter Energy™ - Self -Abusive are afraid to live on their own.

Are you mainly in Daughter Energy™? If so, are you aware of your behaviors that demonstrate this? What are these behaviors? If you are in Daughter Energy™, do you have any desire to move out of that energy and way of being? If not, how does Daughter Energy™ serve you?

Are you in Daughter Energy™ - Entitled with some people and Daughter Energy™ – Self-Abusive with others? If so, with whom are you in Daughter Energy™ -Entitled? With whom are you in Daughter Energy™ -Self-Abusive?

What triggers you to move from one side of the energy to the other?

Do you expect people to be responsible for your happiness? If so, has this helped you feel happy? Do you find people let you down frequently? Who lets you down the most? Would you feel more powerful if you were responsible for your happiness? If so, why? If not, why not? Be honest with yourself.

Do you feel good about taking advantage of people? Do you expect people to change their plans to suit your needs? If so, why?

Would you like to start feeling more powerful within and begin to know that you can take care of yourself? Do you believe that you can take care of yourself? If not, why not?

Who in your life is mainly in Daughter Energy™? Whom do you become when you interact with these females? How do you feel when you are interacting with theses females? Have you been able to state that your time and needs matter around these females? If not, why not?

Which males in your life cause you to be in Daughter Energy™? How do you feel when you are interacting with these males? How do you want to feel when interacting with these males?

What was your biggest awareness or ah-ha from this chapter?

Did you release the unsupportive thoughts, feelings, beliefs, subconscious programming or patterns that came up for you as you worked through this chapter? If not, why not? Don't cheat yourself by skipping this step.

Chapter 5

❖　　❖　　❖

What is Woman Energy™?

A woman in Woman Energy™ knows what her needs and desires are and she is capable of meeting her needs and pursuing her desires. This isn't a selfish energy, but a self-full energy. A woman in Woman Energy™ is present in her own life and she is fully engaged in it. Women in both Mother Energy™ and Daughter Energy™ are neither present nor engaged in their own lives.

Key points in this chapter:

*   Woman Energy™ is neither selfish nor does it allow others to be selfish.
*   A woman in Woman Energy™ collaborates with others and does so with ease.
*   She embodies the energy of joy, allowing, receiving and intuition.
*   She feels safe in the world.
*   This woman is authentic and magnetic to be around.
*   Unlike the giving to prove energy of Mother Energy™ and the taking energy of Daughter Energy™, Woman Energy™ is "gifting and receiving" energy.
*   She has nothing to prove and she isn't interested in fulfilling someone else's requirement that she prove herself.
*   Instead of giving to prove, she gifts everything. A woman in Woman Energy™ gifts her time, energy, attention, focus, talents and abilities.

* Gifting is free of attachment. When you gift something, you release it and it is free to be received or not. There is no expectation of getting when you gift.
* Having dreams and desires is an important part of the human experience.
* Women in both Mother Energy™ and Daughter Energy™ are victims of their circumstances, the demands of others and being shut out of other people's lives. There is no power in being a victim.
* Women in Woman Energy™ don't see themselves as victims. They see themselves as powerful, influential, purposeful and self-directed.
* As women, we thrive with oxytocin flowing through our bodies. This leads to a "tend and befriend" state and allows us to feel safe, connected and trusting.
* A woman in Woman Energy™ is in an oxytocin state. She is calm and centered and her physiology supports this.
* A woman in Woman Energy™ lives in the energy of ease. Ease is an overarching energy that allows you to stay out of struggle.
* Woman Energy™ is expansive energy. It is a self-full energy.
* Mother Energy™ and Daughter Energy™ are constrictive energies.
* A woman in Woman Energy™ is in an optimal balance of her feminine and masculine energies.
* Feminine energy is the flow. Masculine energy provides the structure.
* Think of boundaries as the structure that allows your flow to be directed in ways that support your highest version of yourself.
* Mother Energy™ women generally achieve through force.
* Force is an adrenaline state that leaves women feeling depleted, bitchy, defeated and exhausted.
* Daughter Energy™ women require the structure provided or imposed by their circumstances or others to get things done. This structure is often resented and resisted.
* Resentment and resistance are adrenaline states.
* A woman in Woman Energy™ has sufficient structure for her energy to flow optimally and she has sufficient flow for her life to move forward well.

What was your reaction when you read about Woman Energy™ in The Thriving Woman's Guide to Setting Boundaries? Does Woman Energy™ feel powerful to you? If so, why? If not, why not? Does this energy feel like it is your natural essence?

Does it feel like being in Woman Energy™ will make your life easier? If so, why? If not, why not? Do you believe it is possible to be in Woman Energy™? If so, why? If not, why not? Do you believe that being in Woman Energy™ would make a difference in your life? If so, why? If not, why not? Do you intuitively know that Woman Energy™ is who you naturally are?

Does Woman Energy™ feel like some kind of ideal? If so, why? If not, why not? Does Woman Energy™ feel like just one more thing to aim for?

Whom do you know in Woman Energy™? How does it feel to be around these females? How does their energy feel? Do you want to feel this way yourself?

Do you believe true security comes from being able to meet your own needs? If yes, why? If not, why not? What intention do you have for your children, regardless of their ages?

Do you desire to live in the energy of ease? What does this mean to you?

What was your biggest awareness or ah-ha from this chapter?

Did you release the unsupportive thoughts, feelings, beliefs, subconscious programming or patterns that came up for you as you worked through this chapter? If not, why not? Don't cheat yourself by skipping this step.

Chapter 6

❖   ❖   ❖

Mother Energy™, Daughter Energy™, Woman Energy™ and Boundaries

Boundaries can be thought of as your purse. Mother Energy™ - Taken Advantage of says, "I will carry your purse because I don't have the right to say no to your expectation of this." Mother Energy™ - Intrusive, says, "I will carry your purse because I don't think that you can do that for yourself."

Daughter Energy™ - Entitled, says, "I expect you to carry my purse because I am entitled to this and I am too lazy or disinterested or important to carry my own purse." Daughter Energy™ - Self-Abusive, says, "You have to carry my purse because I am so fractured that I can't carry it myself."

Woman Energy™ says, "I will carry my purse. You will carry your own age-appropriate purse or gym bag. I will help you if I have the resources available - time, energy, money, attention units, etc. - if you are experiencing a burden or crisis, and if doing so fills me up because I am able to gift my time, energy, attention, money or other resources. I don't do this out of obligation or out of resentment."

If you think about boundaries and setting boundaries from this perspective, you will have a framework that gives you a very clear way to decide whose purse you are carrying and why. When you are in Woman Energy™ and you are carrying your own purse and allowing and expecting everyone else to carry their own age-appropriate purse or gym bag, you are in a very "powerful within" mindset. This mindset is the mindset of true security.

Key points of this chapter:

*   Evaluate every request, behavior, interaction, relationship or experience to see where that would put you with regards to your purse. Will this require you to carry someone else's purse or gym bag? Will it require or demand someone else to carry your purse? Are you assisting someone or are you carrying them or taking over their life?
*   The point of establishing boundaries is to stand in Woman Energy™ at all times.
*   Woman Energy™ becomes the Master Boundary. It contains everything you are responsible for including your physical requirements, your feelings, your likes and dislikes, your desires and dreams, and your truth. You feel secure because you know that you can fully meet your own needs.
*   You value yourself enough to develop trust in yourself and develop mastery.
*   You take care of for yourself what you would normally expect others to take care of for you.
*   Standing in your truth gives others permission to stand in their truth.
*   There is no guilt because you are standing in the essence of who you naturally are – self-sufficient, powerful within and truly secure.
*   You see yourself as secure. You see others as competent and capable of self-sufficiency.
*   You respect your time, your energy, your resources and your dreams.
*   From the day your children are born, you see them becoming self-sufficient and having the ultimate security – being able to meet their own needs.
*   You encourage your children to carry their own purses or gym bags. You encourage them to find solutions to their problems. You don't expect them to carry your purse.
*   You have the power within to protect your time, your energy, your resources, your truth and your dreams. You are not counting on or demanding that someone else do this for you. As well, you are not taking over someone else's life to do it for him or her.
*   You do not allow yourself to intrude into other people's lives. You are a full participant in your own life.
*   This circle, this essence, this energy is the Master Boundary. Everything within it is yours. Everything outside of it is not yours.
*   Woman Energy™ encapsulates all of the aspects of boundaries. It holds the physical, mental, emotional, psychological, psychic and spiritual spaces and contains all of your responsibilities.
*   With Woman Energy™ as the Master Boundary, joy is not only possible but it is a given. Being in joy is truly your soul's reason for you being in human form.

Have you started to pay attention to how you are being as you go throughout your day? What have you noticed?

Have you started to pay attention to the people, activities and interactions that are trying to pull you out of Woman Energy™? If so, who are these people? What are these activities and interactions?

Why do you allow these people, activities and interactions to pull you out of Woman Energy™? Is it that you are just starting to become aware of these? Or, do you have some kind of belief that tells you that you need to be in Mother Energy™ or Daughter Energy™? If you have some beliefs around this, what are these beliefs?

Are you ready to change and become Woman Energy™? If so, why? If not, why not?

What is your WHY for moving into Woman Energy™? Does it feel like it has a lot of energy behind it? Or, does it feel more like a wish? Explain.

Who is trying to persuade you to remain in Mother Energy™ or Daughter Energy™? What is their motive for this? How does that make you feel?

If you are mainly in Mother Energy™ - Taken Advantage of, are you ready to get your life back? If so, why? If not, why not? Is this a scary thought? If so, why?

Do you believe you will be letting people down if you don't continue to take care of everything for everyone? If so, whom are you letting down and how? Does enabling others to be irresponsible for their own lives make you a better person?

Is it exciting to start focusing on what lights you up? Are you afraid that you have no idea what lights you up? Are you so numb that nothing lights you up? Do you want to change this?

If you are in Mother Energy™ - Intrusive, are you ready to focus on your own life? If so, why? If not, why not? Is your life worth focusing on? If so, why? If not, why not? Are you afraid people will be angry with you if you stop doing everything for them or stop bailing them out of their mess? Is their anger more important than your well-being?

If you are in Daughter Energy™, are you ready to step up and be responsible for yourself? This is one of the key characteristics of a woman in Woman Energy™? If so, why? If not, why not? Do you believe you can be responsible for yourself?

What was your biggest awareness or ah-ha from this chapter?

Did you release the unsupportive thoughts, feelings, beliefs, subconscious program-ming or patterns that came up for you as you worked through this chapter? If not, why not? Don't cheat yourself by skipping this step.

Section Two

Boundaries and Living Life On Your Terms

Chapter 7

✦　　✦　　✦

Is Guilt Necessary?

*G*uilt seems to be an epidemic these days, especially for women. It seems like we are supposed to feel guilty for just about everything. Even worse, we feel we are supposed to feel guilty if we feel that we aren't feeling guilty enough.

Key points in this chapter:

* There are two kinds of guilt. The first is "appropriate guilt". This guilt serves as a moral and behavioral compass.
* The second type is "inappropriate or unhealthy guilt". This is what we feel when we believe other people feel we should be doing things differently.
* We fling this into the future.
* This is a really big distraction that keeps you from doing what your heart and your soul are longing for you to do.
* We fear losing approval or attention or acceptance.
* Guilt is like a "should". It kind of feels like crap.
* You can't live a fulfilled life if you are crapping all over yourself.
* Women use guilt to hide out from living a fulfilling life.
* We use guilt on others to prevent them from living a fulfilling life.
* Guilt is a contractive energy that gives us permission to remain stuck and unhappy.

* Guilt is a choice in that you can choose to stay in the emotion of guilt, or you can choose to move out of it and possibly remain out if it.
* Change your programming around this. Guilt is often an automatic response we drop into because we are expected to feel this way and because it is a part of our subconscious programming.
* Choosing to step out of guilt is an operating instruction for *you* and it is something you require to have a boundary around.
* Guilt is a lower vibrating emotion that keeps you from being the greatest version of yourself.
* Moving out of this emotion is a powerful way to move your life forward.
* A woman in Woman Energy™ understands the importance of reprogramming her subconscious mind so that it supports the emotions she chooses to feel so that she can get out of and stay out of guilt.
* There is no space in her life for guilt.
* She has nothing to prove and she doesn't require the approval of others.
* A woman in Woman Energy™ understands that she has the right to live her life on her terms.

Do you feel guilty often? Daily? Weekly? What do you feel guilty about?

Are you a bad person if you don't feel guilt in specific situations? If so, why? List these situations and who is involved in them. How would you like to respond in the future to situations that would normally cause you to feel guilt?

Was guilt used on you when you were growing up? If so, how, where and by whom? What did you learn from this? Do you use guilt on others now? On whom? How does this make you feel?

Do you feel guilty if you say no to something? If yes, are there particular people that make you feel this way? Why is this? Would you like to stop feeling guilty? Be honest with yourself. You can't change what you won't acknowledge.

Do you feel guilty for wanting to pursue your own dreams and desires? What are these dreams and desires? Why do you feel guilty for wanting them to be fulfilled?

Do you understand that guilt is a contractive energy that gives you permission to remain stuck and unhappy? Do you want to remain stuck and unhappy? If so, why? Be honest with yourself. You can't change what you won't acknowledge.

Do you believe feeling guilt is a choice? If so, why? If not, why not? Do you use guilt as a way to hide out from living a fulfilling life? If so, why?

Do you use guilt on others to prevent them from living a fulfilled life? If so, on whom? Why? How does this make you feel?

Do you need your children to feel guilty for everything you have done for them and every sacrifice you have made for them? If so, why? How does this really make you feel? Are you making them pay the price for your unfulfilled dreams?

Is guilt an automatic response for you? If so, were you aware of this prior to reading The Thriving Woman's Guide to Setting Boundaries? Are you aware of it when it is happening? Are you aware of what triggers you to feel guilt? List these triggers.

Is guilt the emotion that keeps you at your mother's level of happiness? If so, were you aware of this prior to reading The Thriving Woman's Guide to Setting Boundaries? Do you want to change this?

Is guilt the socially expected reaction to everything and you simply feel this way to fit in with society's expectations? If so, were you aware of this prior to reading The Thriving Woman's Guide to Setting Boundaries? Are you willing to choose a different reaction?

Do you need the approval of others? If so, why? From whom? What happens if you don't get their approval?

Are you ready to change your subconscious programming around guilt? What are some of those programs?

What was your biggest awareness or ah-ha from this chapter?

Did you release the unsupportive thoughts, feelings, beliefs, subconscious programming or patterns that came up for you as you worked through this chapter? If not, why not? Don't cheat yourself by skipping this step.

Chapter 8

What Does Stress Have to Do With Boundaries?

Chronic stress is bad for your health. It puts you at risk of high blood pressure, heart disease and even death. However, picking up on someone else's stress may be significantly more harmful. Chronic vicarious anxiety could have a greater effect on you than direct stress.

Remaining stressed is the selfish behavior that causes second-hand stress to those you love. If you set boundaries so that you are less stressed, everyone around you will benefit. Also, if you continue to keep people in your life who choose to live chronically stressed, know that this stress is contagious and is harming you.

Key points in this chapter:

* You have the right to limit your exposure to a chronically stressed person. This isn't a selfish act. It is a self-full act that benefits you and those around you.
* It isn't selfish to give yourself space from the demanding drama queen or king.
* If you are this demanding, drama-filled person, stop being that way. Your stress is making other people sick.
* You don't owe anyone an explanation for your boundaries.
* You have the right to protect yourself in whatever way is necessary.

* You have the right to not be in an environment that puts you at risk.
* People wear stress as a badge of honor.
* Because so much of who we are is tied into how hard we work, it is very difficult to reduce stress.
* What most people hear when someone tells them that they are too stressed is that they aren't handling things well.
* To reduce stress long term you have to know how you feel and what you believe about stress.
* If you have had enough of being stressed, you will let it go more easily. You will establish the boundaries necessary to reduce your stress.

Do you feel stressed all the time? If so, can you pinpoint why? What causes you to feel stressed? Is it specific to certain people, situations or experiences? Identify these. Is it generalized?

Do you believe remaining stressed is a selfish behavior? If so, why? If not, why not?

Do you believe stress is contagious? Have you ever picked up someone else's stress? Were you aware of it at the time? How did you know? How did it feel to you? Do you avoid this person now? If not, why not?

Are you interested in reducing your stress? If so, why? If not, why not? Be honest with yourself.

Do you feel like you need to prove to others that you "can handle it" and take on more to show that? If so, for whom do you need to do this? How do you feel when you do this?

Would you be okay if you handled less? If so, why? If not, why not? Be honest with yourself. Would you be okay if you handed over some tasks to others for them to handle? If yes, why? If not, why not? Do you believe these tasks would get done if you didn't do them?

What would your life be like if you had less stress? Can you imagine this? Do you believe it is even possible? Whatever you believe is true for you.

Do you keep people in your life who choose to live chronically stressed? If yes, who are these people? Why do you keep them in your life?

Do you believe you have the right to limit your exposure to people who choose to live chronically stressed? If so, why? If not, why not? Are you this chronically stressed person? If so, are you aware that this is harming others? Do you want to change this? If so, why? If not, why not?

Do you feel threatened when people say you are stressed? If so, who are these people? Why do you feel threatened?

Do you feel you have the right to protect yourself from stress and stressful people in whatever way is necessary? If so, why? If not, why not? Have you done so in the past? If not, what stopped you? What stops you now? Do you have the right to not be in an environment that puts you at risk? If not, why not?

Do you wear stress as a badge of honor? Be honest with yourself. You can't change what you won't acknowledge. If so, why? Are you seeking approval? If so from whom? How does this validate you?

Are you ready to establish the boundaries necessary to reduce your stress? If so, why? If not, why not?

What was your biggest awareness or ah-ha from this chapter?

Did you release the unsupportive thoughts, feelings, beliefs, subconscious programming or patterns that came up for you as you worked through this chapter? If not, why not? Don't cheat yourself by skipping this step.

Chapter 9

❖ ❖ ❖

How Does Pleasure Fit With Boundaries?

*T*he number one thing a woman can do to balance her hormones is to increase pleasure in her life. Pleasure is defined as the state of feeling of being pleased. It is also enjoyment or satisfaction derived from what is to one's liking, gratification or delight. How much better would your life be if you filled each day with activities, interactions and experiences that please you?

Key points of this chapter:

* We can experience pleasure in many ways.
* Think about the things you enjoy and how they increase your feelings of pleasure.
* Daughter Energy™ women can't infuse pleasure into their day because they are always expecting others to do this for them. This leads to terrible disappointments.
* You have to know what pleases you and you need to be the one who infuses these pleasures into your day and your life.
* As you increase the amount of pleasure in your day and your hormones start to become more balanced, your mood will improve. As your mood improves, everyone around you will be positively impacted.
* We have bought into the notion of "no pain, no gain". This is a harmful belief, especially for women. This mindset says that to move forward, it must hurt first.
* We can only build up our capacity for pleasure. This builds up a reservoir of energy we can use in times of difficulty.

* We cannot, nor should we want to, build up our capacity for pain.
* If you increase your capacity for experiencing pleasure, you will be able to cope more easily when something painful happens and you will be able to recover faster when the painful experience is over.
* If your life is devoid of pleasure, you don't have much energy available to deal with life's valleys.
* Do at least one thing every day that pleases you.
* Build up a reservoir of pleasure and delight. This will keep you centered when life knocks you off balance.
* There is pleasure in carrying your own purse.
* There is pleasure in not getting stuck carrying someone else's purse or gym bag.
* There is pleasure in saying, "This activity pleases me and when you do that, it displeases me."
* There is pleasure in being fully responsible for yourself.
* There is pleasure in expecting and requiring everyone to have age-appropriate responsibility for themselves.

What was your definition of pleasure before reading this chapter in The Thriving Woman's Guide to Setting Boundaries? How do you define it now?

Are you open to adding pleasure to your day? If so, why? If not, why not? Are you worthy of adding pleasure to your day? If not, why not? How do you think adding pleasure to your day would add to your life?

What kinds of things, experiences, and activities please you? List them. Have you allowed yourself to think about this? If not, why not?

Are you afraid of the judgment of others if you start doing things that please you? If so, from whom? Why does this matter to you?

Are you afraid the people around you will judge you if you aren't struggling through the daily grind? Who are these people? Why do they matter?

How much better would your life be if you filled each day with activities, interactions and experiences that please you? Can you even imagine this?

Do you believe in "no pain, no gain"? If so, why? If not, why not? Do you believe you can and should build up your capacity for pain? If so, how does this feel to you? Is this supportive for you?

Do you believe you can and should build up your capacity for pleasure? If so, how does this feel to you? How would you know when you have done this?

What pleasures have you started to infuse into your day? What other pleasures would you like to infuse into your day? What stops you from doing this?

What was your biggest awareness or ah-ha from this chapter?

Did you release the unsupportive thoughts, feelings, beliefs, subconscious programming or patterns that came up for you as you worked through this chapter? If not, why not? Don't cheat yourself by skipping this step.

Chapter 10

❖   ❖   ❖

Is it Selfish to Say NO?

*I*t is possible to provide care that would be deeply pleasing to you**.** It is also possible that provid-ing care would make you incredibly resentful and hostile. If you can say yes to providing care because it pleases you, then everyone benefits. If you say yes to providing care but in doing so makes you incredibly hostile, then no one benefits. If you said yes in this situation, everyone loses.

Key points in this chapter:

* You have the right and the permission to say no to a request or expectation. Know, to your core, that you are not a bad person for doing so.
* If you do say yes you don't have to do all of the work yourself. You can and should ask for sup-port from others.
* Asking is critical. People aren't mind readers.
* Asking for support and assistance is truly a sign of strength and an acknowledgment that you want to honor yourself during this trying time.
* A woman in Woman Energy™ doesn't expect to do it all by herself.
* She can receive support without feeling obligated to give in return.
* She isn't a taker and she isn't expecting people to carry her so when she needs support and as-sistance, she is free to receive this and gifts support freely.
* She carries her own purse and doesn't take advantage of people. However, she has their backs in a way that doesn't leave her depleted.
* Assisting others in a time of need simply means that you lighten their purse or gym bag. It doesn't mean you carry them.

How did you feel about saying no before you read this chapter in The Thriving Woman's Guide to Setting Boundaries?

How do you feel about saying no now? Do you believe you have the right to say no? If so, why? What has changed for you? If not, why not?

Is everything your responsibility to take care of? If so, why? Is it really true that everything is your responsibility to take care of? How would you really feel if everything wasn't your responsibility to take care of?

How would you actually feel if you said no? Are you letting people down? Are you afraid "it" won't get done properly if you don't do it yourself?

Did Amy's story help you understand that saying yes often has long-lasting negative consequences? If so, how did it help you? If not, why not?

What would you like to say no to? List these. What stops you from saying no?

Whom are you betraying if you say no? Why do you feel you are betraying this (these) person (people)?

What are you not saying yes to that would enhance your life?

Do you believe it is selfish to say no to something you have absolutely no interest in doing? If so, why? If not, why not?

What subconscious programming would you need to release for you to believe you have the right to say no to providing care (or anything else for that matter)?

What was your biggest awareness or ah-ha from this chapter?

Did you release the unsupportive thoughts, feelings, beliefs, subconscious programming or patterns that came up for you as you worked through this chapter? If not, why not? Don't cheat yourself by skipping this step.

Chapter 11

❖   ❖   ❖

Mother Energy™, Daughter Energy™ and Your Health

There is a really good reason to move out of either Mother Energy™ or Daughter Energy™ and into Woman Energy™. Being in either Mother Energy™ or Daughter Energy™ can contribute to health issues.

Key points in this chapter:

* Everything is energy and everything has a vibration and a resonance.
* Every organ in your body has a healthy vibration. Anything that goes on in your body that has a lower vibration can cause the vibrations of your organs, and everything else in your body for that matter, to decrease.
* Lower vibrations in your body lead to dis-ease and potentially to disease.
* Your thoughts are energy. Your emotions are energy. Lower vibrating thoughts and emotions cause your body to be unhappy.

Do you refuse to nourish yourself physically? Mentally? Emotionally? Psychologically? Spiritually? If so, why for each area? Are you malnourished in all areas? As you reflect on this, how does this make you feel? Why have you allowed this?

Do you over-mother? If so, is this limited to just your children? Do you over-mother everyone? Do people appreciate your over-mothering? Does it feel intrusive and invalidating to them? Would you want someone to over-mother you? As you reflect on all of this, how does this make you feel?

Are you overprotective? If so, is it just with your children? With others? Why do you feel you need to overprotect? Do these individuals appreciate it? Are these individuals deficient in some way? What does this behavior prevent you from doing in your own life?

Do you act and react like a little kid? If so, how and why? How does this serve you?

Do you suffer from any of the conditions I listed in The Thriving Woman's Guide to Setting Boundaries? If so, list them.

Do you feel rejected by someone or something? If so, by what or whom? How is this showing up in your life? How is this showing up in your body?

Are you carrying around hurts? If so, how are these showing up in your life? How are these showing up in your body?

Are you full of fear? Is this specific to certain people, events or experiences? If so, list them. Is this generalized fear? If so, when did this start? Are you ready to move beyond this fear? If so, why? If not, why not? Do you feel you need to hang on to this fear to keep yourself safe? If so, is this really keeping you safe?

Do you believe people will (are) take (taking) advantage of you? If so, who is doing this? Why do you allow this?

Do you believe people are too sensitive? Is it some people? All people? If so, why?

Do you do things to gain the approval of yourself? Others? Do you always give yourself approval? What if others don't approve? What do you do about it and how do you feel?

Do you have feelings of guilt? Always? Sometimes? Over what? Do you feel guilty if you don't feel guilty enough?

Do you have feelings of shame? Are you ready to release these feelings? If not, why not? Are you worthy and deserving of releasing these feelings? If not, why not?

Do you have feelings of wrongful pride (an over-inflated sense of yourself)? If so, regarding what? How do you feel about yourself when you feel this way?

Do you have feelings of envy? With certain people? Over certain activities? In general? If so, why? How does this make you feel?

Do you believe that people must think well of you for you to be okay? Why does their opinion matter to you? What if they don't think well of you? How does that make you feel? What do you do so they think well of you?

What would you like to stop doing but feel you can't or won't because you believe people will think poorly of you?

Do you engage in the pattern of manipulation? Be honest here. Is it with certain people? Everyone? How do you feel about this?

Are you lazy? Be honest here. This is just for your awareness. How does this make you feel?

Do you feel entitled? If so, to what do you feel entitled?

Do you feel helpless or behave helplessly? In all situations? In certain situations? List these. Do you feel helpless or behave helplessly with certain people? With all people? With whom do you feel helpless? Why?

Do you believe "I can't do it?" If so, why? What evidence do you have that says this is true?

Do you believe "I'm not capable?" If so, based on what experiences?

Do you believe others should do "it" (whatever that is) for you? If so, why? Why can't you do "it" for yourself?

Do you believe "it's not fair?" If so, what's not fair? Life? Someone else's life? Something else? Why is "it" not fair?

Do you engage in the behavior of deceiving others? If so, is this limited to certain individuals? Or, do you deceive all people at some point? Why do you do this? How does this make you feel?

Do you often give up when doing something? If so, why?

Are you unforgiving? If so, with whom and toward what?

Do you feel insignificant? If so, is this all the time? Do you believe you are insignificant? If so, is this all the time? Is this with specific experiences? Is this with certain people? Where is this being expressed in your body?

Do you feel resentment? If so, is this with specific people? Specific situations? Where do you feel this in your body?

Do you feel jealous often? If so, why? Of whom? Where is this being expressed in your body?

Do you believe you are unlovable? If so, why? Where do you feel this in your body?

Do you believe you are flawed? If so, why? Where is this being expressed in your body?

Do you shut out the world for self-protection? If so, why? Can you see how this would actually make you weaker? How is this being expressed in or on your body?

Do you feel powerless? If so, is this in certain situations? Is it all the time? Where do you feel this in your body?

Are you filled with anger? If so, is this generalized across your life? Is this in certain situations? With certain people? Where do you feel this in your body? Do you feel entitled to feel angry? If so, how does this serve you?

Are you filled with hostility? If so, is this all the time? Is this with specific individuals? In specific situations? Where do you feel this in your body?

Do you believe that carrying your own purse is necessary for your own well-being? If so, why? If not, why not?

Do you believe that requiring others to carry their own age-appropriate purses or gym bags is essential for your well-being? Do you believe you have the right to require this? Are you being mean if you do this?

Do you believe that having the sense of true security of being able to take care of your own needs is essential to your own well-being? If so, why? If not, why not?

Do you believe that allowing and requiring everyone to take care of their own age-appropriate needs is essential to your well-being? If so, why? Are you being mean if you require this? If so, why? Are you being selfish if you require this? If so, why? Are you harming these individuals if you do this? If so, how? What beliefs do you have around this that are preventing you from doing so?

What was your biggest awareness or ah-ha from this chapter?

Did you release the unsupportive thoughts, feelings, beliefs, subconscious program-ming or patterns that came up for you as you worked through this chapter? If not, why not? Don't cheat yourself by skipping this step.

Section Three

Key Areas of Your Life That Require Boundaries

Chapter 12

❖   ❖   ❖

Should You Set Boundaries With Your Children?

When children have boundaries set for them and parents set limits on their children's behaviors, then children understand that they are loved. When you, as a parent, set limits on your children's behaviors, but not, however, on their dreams, you are letting your children know that you care enough to do that and that they matter enough for you to care. The opposite of this is true as well. If you don't set limits on your children's behaviors and don't have expectations for them, children interpret this to mean that you don't care enough to do that and they don't matter enough for you to do so.

Key points in this chapter:

* A woman in Woman Energy™ understands that not only does setting boundaries with her children, young or grown up, help them feel loved and valued, it is also a way for her children to balance their masculine and feminine energies.
* Your lack of boundaries for your children impacts others, not just you.
* Don't raise your daughters to be princesses. They become someone else's burden later on.
* Don't raise your sons to be princes. This results in grown-up boys.
* No matter the age of your children always have the intention of these people growing into self-sufficient adults, even if they are adults already.

* It is never too late to establish boundaries with your children. Even if you didn't have boundaries with your children when they were young, you can establish them now with your grown-up children.

* Having no expectations of your children is significantly more damaging to them than having big expectations for them.

* When you have no expectations of and for your children and you do everything for them, subconsciously they understand this to mean that you don't believe they can do anything.

* When everything is done for children and they aren't allowed to try things for themselves, they start to believe that everything needs to be absolutely perfect the first time they do try something because you have instilled in them that failure is not an option.

* Children are constantly seeking boundaries and limits. You are not harming them if you have boundaries and limits on their behavior. Limits and boundaries make them feel safe, loved and cared for.

* As important as it is to have expressed boundaries and limits for your children's behavior, it is equally important to have boundaries around your behavior and expectations with your children.

* Do not expect your children to parent you. It is your job as their parent to parent them, not the other way around.

* Do not expect your children to be responsible for your emotions, especially for your happiness. This is your responsibility and only you can make you happy.

* Do not live your life through your children. You are required, as a healthy, vibrant adult, to have and pursue your own dreams and desires and you need to expect and give space to your children to have and pursue their own dreams and desires.

* Do not make your children feel they aren't smart enough to figure things out on their own.

* Do not burden your children with all of your problems.

* A woman in Woman Energy™ establishes boundaries for her children, whether young or grown-up, because she knows that this is in the best interest of her children and herself.

New Insight

Did you know that children don't *start to develop* reasoning skills until they are about 16 – 17 years old? Did you also know that reasoning skills aren't generally fully developed until about the age of 25?

Reasoning is the ability to predict an outcome from an action. If you have reasoning skills it means that you can figure out "if this, then that." For example, if I do this (say this, behave this way, take this course of action), then that will happen (the outcome will be x, y or z). It means that you can figure out cause and effect.

Often when I mention reasoning skills to parents they get angry at me for implying that their kids aren't smart. Actually, reasoning skills have nothing to do with intelligence. Reasoning is a psychological development process, not an intelligence factor. If you have ever watched the TV show, "The Big Bang Theory", you will see this principle in action. The character of Sheldon Cooper is highly intelligent but he often can't determine an outcome of his actions and he is caught off guard by what actually happens.

What all of this means for your kids is that they don't have the psychological development to make sound decisions for themselves until they are at least in their late teens. They require you to set boundaries for them so that they have the structure to navigate the world safely until they develop the ability to reason. You wouldn't let them figure out how to cross the street all by themselves without any rules to get there safely would you? Then why would you let them navigate the world without setting boundaries for them?

New Insight

Here are five key reasons to set boundaries with your children. The ones marked with * were not mentioned in *The Thriving Woman's Guide to Setting Boundaries*.

1. Boundaries make your children feel safe.* Your children's world feels very unsafe if they have no idea what and where the limits of their behaviors are. Your kids will push and push until they find the snap-back point. This point makes them feel safe. Setting boundaries for your children makes them feel safe.

2. Boundaries make your kids feel loved.* When you set boundaries for your kids and make their world feel safe, they feel loved.

3. Boundaries make your kids feel like you care. If you set boundaries with your kids, it tells them that you care enough to do so and that they matter enough for you to care.

4. Your kids expect them. Everyone expects you to have boundaries. At a subconscious level, everyone is unsettled by the lack of boundaries and everyone's interactions are easier and smoother when you have them. When you don't have boundaries with your kids, they feel unsettled.

5. Boundaries give your kids an out with their friends.* It is very difficult for your children to say no to their friends. If you have already set out the limits for their behaviors, they can blame you when they need to say no to their friends but don't really know how to do so otherwise. Your kids can simply say, "My parents won't let me" to their friends. This makes it easy for your children to say no without having to say no.

Do you believe that when children have boundaries set for them and parents set limits on their children's behaviors, these children understand that they are loved? If so, why? If not, why not?

Do you believe that when you set limits on your children's behaviors you are letting them know that you care enough to do that and that they matter enough for you to care? If so, why? If not, why not?

Does it feel mean to set boundaries for your children? If so, why? If not, why not? Is it mean to require your children, under-aged or grown, to become self-sufficient so that they have the true security of being able to take care of their own needs as adults?

Do you believe that if you don't set limits on your children's behaviors and you don't have expectations for them, your children will interpret this to mean that you don't care enough to do that and they don't matter enough for you to do so? If so, why? If not, why not?

Do you believe that your lack of boundaries for your children impacts others? If so, why? If not, why not?

Are you open to setting boundaries with your under-aged children? Grown children? If so, why now? Do you believe you have the right to do so?

If you are carrying your under-aged children's age-appropriate purses or gym bags when would be a good time for your children to start carrying them? Do you want to carry them forever? Is it helping your children to have true security as an adult if you carry their purses or gym bags forever?

Are you carrying your grown children's purses or gym bags? Is it mean of you to require them to carry their own purses or gym bags? Is it selfish of you to require them to carry their own purses or gym bags? If you are still carrying their purses or gym bags how long do you want to continue to do this? What else could you be doing with this energy?

Do you not trust your parenting? Are your grown children deficient in some way that makes it impossible for them to carry their own purses or gym bags?

Are you messing around in your grown children's purses or gym bags?

❖   ❖   ❖

Do you believe it is selfish to allow your children, under-aged or grown, to develop the true security of being able to take care of their own needs? If so, why is it selfish to allow your children to develop true security? Is it selfish of you to never allow your children, under-aged or grown, to have true security?

❖   ❖   ❖

What are you afraid will happen if you don't carry your children's purses or gym bags? Be honest with yourself here.

What was your biggest awareness or ah-ha from this chapter?

Did you release the unsupportive thoughts, feelings, beliefs, subconscious programming or patterns that came up for you as you worked through this chapter? If not, why not? Don't cheat yourself by skipping this step.

Chapter 13

❖   ❖   ❖

Do You Have the Right to Set Boundaries With Your Husband?

Having boundaries with your husband/partner is critical if you want to live a joyful life together. As women, we really struggle in this area of our lives. Most of us believe that we aren't entitled to have boundaries with our husbands or partners.

Key points in this chapter:

* We continue to receive opportunities to set boundaries for ourselves until we establish them.
* It is never too late to establish boundaries and better operating instructions with your husband/partner.
* It is never too late to teach your husband/partner how to treat you.
* A woman in Woman Energy™ requires her husband/partner to be in Man Energy™ because all energy seeks balance.
* There are two sides to Father Energy™. The first side is Father Energy™ - Father Knows Best. He expects to be treated like a king. He is demanding, selfish and narcissistic.
* The other side of Father Energy™ is Father Energy™ - Taken Advantage of. He over-commits and he can't say no. He is exhausted and depleted and feels he has let everyone down.
* There are two sides to Son Energy™. The first side is Son Energy™ - The Son. This grown man is still desperately seeking the approval of his mother and father.

* The other side of Son Energy™ is Son Energy™ - Indifferent. He has been raised to be "The Little Prince". He is narcissistic and believes that his needs are all that matter.
* A man in Man Energy™ understands that his role is protector. It is his job to make you feel safe. He understands that when you feel safe, you can thrive.
* A man in Man Energy™ has an optimal balance of masculine and feminine energies.
* The natural essence of a man is to be in Man Energy™. He is strong and confident and he always has your back.
* Men, in general, unless they are narcissistic, are wired to please women. We have to give them the space to do that.
* Start paying attention to the issues that bother you and ask yourself, "Why does this bother me?" Also ask yourself, "How am I contributing to this? and "What outcome do I want if I set a boundary in this area?"
* Pay attention to where your husband/partner has boundaries.
* A compromise is not a healthy choice because you are not choosing this option. You are being forced into this option. It makes you feel like you are giving up a piece of yourself.
* A concession is a healthy response to a situation. It feels open. It feels like you have a choice. If you are the only person in the relationship that is constantly making concessions, then you are settling – settling for less than you deserve, less than you desire.
* Are you saying yes to something just to make or keep your husband/partner (or anyone else for that matter) happy even though this really doesn't work for you? If so, you are compromising.
* Establishing boundaries with your husband/partner is a retraining process. It won't happen overnight and it takes consistency on your part to make it so. Honor yourself enough to stick with it.
* Require your husband/partner to respect you because you respect yourself and require your husband/partner to respect your time because you respect your time.
* You need to show him that you value and respect yourself, you value and respect your time, you value and respect your needs and wants, and you require all of these to be valued and respected by him.
* You are responsible for knowing what you desire to receive in the form of gifts.
* You are worthy of receiving gifts.

Do you believe you have the right to set boundaries with your husband/ partner? If so, why? If not, why not?

Do you have boundaries with your husband or partner in all areas that require boundaries with him? Are there areas that require boundaries but you don't have any? If so, list them. What stops you from having boundaries in this (these) area(s)?

If you really don't have boundaries with your husband/partner, how is he supposed to know your operating instructions? Are you expecting him to guess what your expectations are in any given situation? If so, how is that working for you?

Do you require your husband/partner to be in Man Energy™? Remember, for him to be in Man Energy™, you must be in Woman Energy™. Are you in Woman Energy™? If not, how will your husband/partner be in Man Energy™? Do you want to be in Woman Energy™? If so, why? If not, why not?

Is your husband/partner old enough to carry his own gym bag? If not now, at what age would he be old enough to do so?

Have you started to pay attention to the issues that bother you? What are these issues?

How are you contributing to these issues?

What outcome do you want if you set boundaries in these areas? List these outcomes.

Have you been willing to give up control of these issues if you are in Mother Energy™ - Intrusive with your husband/partner? If not, why not? If not, where is the space for your husband/partner to step up?

Have you been willing to step up and be responsible for things with your husband or partner if you are in Daughter Energy™? If not, what stops you from stepping up?

Do you believe that your time matters? If not, why not? How will your husband/ partner believe your time matters if you don't believe that it does?

Do you believe that your needs matter? If not, why not? How will your husband or partner believe that your needs matter if you don't believe they do?

Do you require your husband or partner to respect your time and your needs? If not, what stops you from requiring this?

Have you paid attention to where your husband or partner has boundaries? What are some of the key areas?

Do you have playtime for yourself scheduled in your calendar? If so, for what? If not, why not? Do you have the right to honor this time as your time? If not, why not? How do you really feel about this?

Do you expect this time to be respected? Do you give it away when something comes up that your husband or partner wants you to handle? If so, why? Are you willing to stop doing this? Does your husband or partner give up his playtime to take care of something you want him to handle?

Are your husband's or partner's needs more important than yours? If so, why? Were you raised to believe that your husband or partner is more important than you are? How does this really make you feel?

Is it selfish to take care of your needs first? If so, why? How do you really feel about this? Are you a better person for taking care of your needs last? What if your needs never get taken care of?

Do you believe that your husband or partner will only like you if you do everything he asks of you and expects from you? If so, how does that really make you feel?

If your husband or partner earns more than you, is he more important than you? If so, how does that make you feel? How does that impact your boundaries?

Are you letting your husband or partner know that if he doesn't do the task he committed to doing he is eroding your trust? If not, how will he know?

Do you believe your husband or partner wants to build or maintain your trust? If not, why not? If so, how does he demonstrate this? Have you ever paid attention to this?

What is your definition of compromise?

Before reading The Thriving Woman's Guide to Setting Boundaries, did you believe compromise was required in relationships? If so, why? How did this make you feel?

Do you compromise with your husband or partner? Are you the one who always gives up something that matters to you? If so, why do you feel you need to do this?

What is your definition of concession?

Would you rather make a compromise or a concession? Why?

Have you started taking responsibility for what you desire in the form of gifts? Do you believe that this is your responsibility? If so, why? If not, why not?

What was your biggest awareness or ah-ha from this chapter?

Did you release the unsupportive thoughts, feelings, beliefs, subconscious programming or patterns that came up for you as you worked through this chapter? If not, why not? Don't cheat yourself by skipping this step.

Chapter 14

Your Boundaries and the Digital World

As women, we often feel overwhelmed by the constant tug to be and remain connected. The digital world seems to a "place" where we really need to set boundaries but don't for fear of missing out or the possibility that we will likely offend others. Often, because we haven't given this area any thought, we simply go along with whatever is the socially accepted way of being without stopping to evaluate how this is working in our lives. Generally, we feel so overwhelmed that we don't have the mental or emotional energy to figure out how all of this really makes us feel. Answering questions around this will help you become clear on what is really going on and how you really feel about this area of your life.

Key points in this chapter:

* If anyone and everyone has full access to you day and night, then you are on-call.
* When people are on-call for work purposes, they get paid for being available and ready to take work-related action for a specified period of time. When you are on-call in your private life, you are giving this time away for free without receiving any form of compensation for your availability.
* You have the right to block out any intrusive person from your digital experience. It is imperative for your well-being that you do so.
* Takers are never concerned with your feelings.

* You have the right to protect your feelings by freeing yourself of harmful people. You need to help your children do the same.
* A woman in Woman Energy™ doesn't waste endless hours on social media. She is very protective of her time.
* She feels a whole lot better about herself when she has interactions on these sites with people who lift her up and she eliminates all interactions with people who drag her down.
* She has boundaries around when and with whom she responds on social media.
* She doesn't give everyone in the world access to her.
* She shuts her devices off every evening.

What kind of boundaries do you have for your electronic devices and the digital world? Do you feel overwhelmed with the digital world?

Had you given this any thought prior to reading The Thriving Woman's Guide to Setting Boundaries? Do you believe you need boundaries for your digital experience? If so, why? If not, why not?

Do you have limits for your under-age children regarding their electronic devices? If so, what are these? If not, why not?

Do you check your under-aged children's devices to ensure that they aren't inviting in trouble? If you aren't doing this, who is?

Is your phone for your convenience? Or is it for the convenience of everyone who wants to communicate with you? Explain.

Do you give everyone and anyone full access to you day and night? If so, why? How does this make you feel? Were you aware that you are on-call if everyone and anyone can get a hold of you any time of the day or night? How do you feel about being on-call?

Would you feel less stressed if you had boundaries around who can reach you and when? If so, what stops you from setting these boundaries? Would you feel more stressed if you had boundaries around who can reach you and when? If so, why?

Do you have boundaries for when you respond to people's voice mails, texts, updates? If so, what are these boundaries? If not, why not?

Does all of your interaction please you? List the interactions (where, with whom) that please you. List the interactions (where, with whom) that don't please you.

Are there people with whom you need to have less interaction? List them.

Do you feel you have the right to limit this interaction? If not, why not? If so, have you started to limit this interaction? If not, why not?

Does the majority of your social media communication help you feel better about yourself or worse about yourself? If it makes you feel better about yourself, how

kim

does it do this? If it makes you feel worse about yourself, why do you continue to have this communication?

Do you limit whom you interact with on social media? If not, why not? Are you afraid you are missing out on something if you don't follow everyone or provide up-dates for everyone? If so, what are you missing out on? What is this costing you in other areas of your life?

Does everyone you follow or interact with on social media lift you up? Drag you down? With whom do you interact on social media that lifts you up? List them. Who drags you down? List them.

If there are people you interact with on social media that drag you down, why do you continue to interact/follow these people? Do you have the right to stop interacting with them?

Do you find that instead of actually living your life, you spend your time trying to look like you are living your life in a way that appeals to your audience? If so, why wouldn't you simply live your life instead of pretending to be doing that?

Are you connected to the digital world but disconnected from those who matter most to you – your husband/partner, children, close friends,? Be honest here. This is purely for your awareness. If so, are you aware that these relationships are at risk? If you are aware, what stops you from being more engaged with these people? Why do you want to risk these relationships?

How many hours a week do you spend on social media? Be honest with yourself. If you aren't sure, start tracking it. Is this an area that you just aren't willing to explore? Be honest with yourself. This is simply for your own knowing.

What are you avoiding or hiding out from in your life that would improve if you gave it the time, energy and attention to it as you do to social media? Is all of this time, energy and attention you give to social media moving your life forward? If so, how? If not, why do you continue with this?

Do you check your phone during the night? If so, why is this important to you? Why is sleeping, which is great self-care, less important to you than waking up to check your phone?

What was your biggest awareness or ah-ha from this chapter?

Did you release the unsupportive thoughts, feelings, beliefs, subconscious programming or patterns that came up for you as you worked through this chapter? If not, why not? Don't cheat yourself by skipping this step.

Chapter 15

❖ ❖ ❖

Do You Have the Right to Pursue Your Dreams and Desires?

As women, we often struggle with the belief that it is selfish to pursue our own dreams and desires. These dreams and desires are the longings of our souls. Why do you suppose we have these longings if we aren't meant to pursue them? To live a fulfilling life, you are required to pursue your dreams and desires. Boundaries are essential for these dreams and desires to become a reality.

Key points in this chapter:

* A woman in Mother Energy™ has no time or space to pursue her dreams and desires and has likely forgotten what they are.
* A woman in Daughter Energy™ often doesn't feel capable of pursuing her dreams and desires or she expects others to make them happen for her.
* A woman in Woman Energy™ understands that to live a fulfilling life she is required to pursue her dreams and desires.
* This requirement is part of your internal operating instructions for *you*.
* Your true purpose for being here on earth is to experience joy.
* Often pursuing our desires and dreams is a matter of timing.
* You never want to have regret about something.

* Regret is a very heavy energy that is difficult to disentangle from and requires a lot of forgiveness of yourself. You are always left wondering what it would have been like if you pursued your desire.

* If you are not pursuing your desires and what is in your heart, you will always believe that everyone else needs to somehow pay for this.

* When we deny ourselves the opportunity to pursue our desires we become filled with resentment, which we believe everyone else is supposed to somehow make up for.

* It is simply healthier for all involved for you to pursue what is in your heart.

* This is not all or nothing. Everything requires balance. Balance requires boundaries. A woman in Woman Energy™ understands this.

* Your biochemistry must be in alignment with your dreams and desires. This allows you to receive them more readily.

* You need to be in an oxytocin state and you need to retrain your body to release oxytocin instead of adrenaline.

* When we are in an oxytocin state we are in a tend and befriend state, which means that we feel an internal state of safety where we are connected to ourselves. This state is important for being grounded and fulfilled as a woman.

* Oxytocin allows us to connect and collaborate, both with our desires and with others. It allows us to trust ourselves and trust our desires.

* The moment our bodies get the "I need to survive" message from our thinking and mental field, the fight or flight response kicks in and the body releases adrenaline. You start thinking, "What's in it for me? It's too late. It's too much. I'm not even sure it is possible. I'm not worth it. I can't do it. What's the point? It will never happen for me."

* Only when we feel safe and are in our bodies do we have the biochemistry to thrive.

* A woman in Woman Energy™ is in an oxytocin state.

* When you are in oxytocin, others feel a sense of trust with you. You are able to respond rather than react to the situation. When you are in an adrenaline state, you feel unsafe and others feel you as unsafe. Adrenaline makes you react to the situation and it makes it impossible for you to respond to the situation.

* Reacting makes you bitchy and makes others perceive you as a bitch. This brings out competition, which makes it virtually impossible for you to move your desires forward.

* A woman in Woman Energy™ understands that pursuing her dreams and desires is purely for the journey, for the joy of mastery.

* Mastery is a state of becoming.
* It takes roughly 10,000 hours for us to develop a skill or activity to the point where we have mastery or unconscious competence with it.
* Adrenaline blocks clarity.
* We have a set amount of attention units each week.
* We have more units available at the beginning of the week and few units remaining at the end of the week.
* A woman in Woman Energy™, as best as she can, schedules important meetings and appointments for the beginning of the week and playtime at the end of the week.
* Don't waste attention units frivolously on Facebook, Twitter, Instagram and the like.
* You must give your dreams and desires some attention units each week, even if the timing isn't right for them to be born now.
* Don't waste attention units with pointless worry.
* The set amount of attention units gets used up easily through decision making. Allow and require everyone in your life to make age-appropriate decisions.
* Don't join committees you have no interest in joining. These will take up attention units that would be better served in a different way.
* Focus on being grounded in your body so that your energy is not all up in your head being consumed with endless thinking and mind chatter.
* To be grounded in your body, bring your energy out of your head and down into your belly, about four fingers below your belly button. This is where your power comes from.
* By having energy in your lower belly, you are now able to be present.
* You need to be present and in your conscious mind to pursue your dreams and desires.

Mentioned throughout this chapter in *The Thriving Woman's Guide to Setting Boundaries* are **ways to increase the oxytocin** in your body. Here are those ways:

The most important point is to decide how you want to live your life. If you believe that it is possible to live your life in oxytocin, know that that is true. Whatever you believe … is true for you.

Focusing on bringing pleasure into your life will help to retrain your brain and your body to release oxytocin. Pleasure is an oxytocin state.

Using better, higher vibrating words will help retrain your brain and body to release oxytocin. For example, when you say, "I am excited …" or "I need …" or "I am anxious to …" or ask "When is it going to happen? these statements and question put you into an adrenaline state. When you say, "I am enthusiastic …" or "I trust …" or "I am eager to …" or "I feel safe that this is coming" these statements put you in an oxytocin state.

Different emotions cause you to release adrenaline or oxytocin. When you feel emotions such as worry, embarrassment, disappointment, rejection, guilt, jealousy, drama or resentment you are in an adrenaline state. When you feel emotions of inspiration, courage, hope, trust, joy and love you are in an oxytocin state.

Increase oxytocin through different forms of touch. Hugging is an excellent way to increase oxytocin. Have at least one hug a day with someone you love and trust. This hug should last at least for 10 seconds.

Receive a massage by someone you trust. This will help you be grounded as well. Being grounded and in your body releases oxytocin. When you are up in your head, you are not grounded, you are not present and you are in an adrenaline state.

Oxytocin is released during orgasm, so having sex with someone you love and trust is a great way to increase oxytocin.

Increase oxytocin through your breath. Inhaling activates the sympathetic nervous system and exhaling activates the parasympathetic nervous system. If you make a pleasurable sound out loud when you exhale slowly, you will activate the release of oxytocin. Allow the inhale to fill your belly then exhale slowly making a pleasurable sound. Do several of these breaths in a row and do them several times a day.

Do you believe you have the right to pursue your dreams and desires? If not, why not?

Do you know what your dreams and desires are? If so, list them. If not, would you like to reconnect with them? Do you believe that it is possible to do so? If not, why not?

If you are a mom, do you feel pursuing your dreams takes something away from your children? If so, how does this do that?

Do you realize that if you aren't pursuing your dreams and desires your children are paying the price for this? How does this get expressed in your life?

Have you let go of or given up on your dreams or desires? If so, what are they? Why have you let them go or given up on them?

How do you feel about this? Are you making others pay for this? Are you filled with resentment over this? Be honest here. You can't change what you won't acknowledge.

Are you living in an adrenaline state? If so, are you open to changing this so that you are in an oxytocin state? Do you believe that this would actually make a difference in your life?

Are you addicted to adrenaline and "back against the wall" type of scenarios? If so, list some of these scenarios. Were you aware of this addiction before you read *The Thriving Woman's Guide to Setting Boundaries?* Was this something you wanted to change?

Are you addicted to cortisol? Are you addicted to negative thinking? What are some of your repetitive negative thoughts? Were you aware of this addiction before you read The Thriving Woman's Guide to Setting Boundaries?

Are you stuck in "I need to survive" thinking? If so, why?

Do you feel safe both in your body and in your pursuit of your dreams and desires? If so, why? If not, why not? Would you know if you were feeling safe in your body? How would that feel to you?

Are you in your body? Do you feel grounded? Do you ever pay attention to this? If not, why not? What is stopping you from feeling grounded?

Do you feel fulfilled? If not, do you know what is stopping you from feeling fulfilled? What would help you feel fulfilled?

Do you feel eager for your dreams and desires to unfold? Do you feel excited for your dreams and desires to unfold? Can you feel the difference in your body? Which one feels better in your body? If you feel neither eager nor excited, imagine what it would feel like to feel eager for your dreams and desires to unfold. Can you even imagine this?

Do you pursue your dreams and desires for the outcome or the journey? If for the outcome, how does this feel in your body? Does this put you in an adrenaline state? Do you have any awareness of that? If for the journey, how does this feel in your body? Which of these feels better to you?

How often are you in your conscious mind? Are you even aware when this happens? Do you generally go through your day in a robotic state? If so, does this feel stressful to you? Would you like to have more presence? What stops you from this?

What was your biggest awareness or ah-ha from this chapter?

Did you release the unsupportive thoughts, feelings, beliefs, subconscious programming or patterns that came up for you as you worked through this chapter? If not, why not? Don't cheat yourself by skipping this step.

Section Four

Becoming Woman Energy™ and Stepping Into the Master Boundary

Chapter 16

✦ ✦ ✦

How Do You Become Woman Energy™?

*W*oven throughout *The Thriving Woman's Guide to Setting Boundaries* are the characteristics of a woman in Woman Energy™. This is our natural way of being. I have brought all these characteristics together in the list below. As you read through them, feel them in your body and identify which ones you naturally embody. For the ones that aren't part of your way of being feel into them. Allow yourself to feel if you have resonance with them and if these characteristics feel like they should be natural for you but there is something, a thought, feeling, belief, subconscious programming or pattern that stops or prevents you from simply being that way. The more you become aware of what is natural for a woman who is centered, grounded and balanced in Woman Energy™ and release what is in the way of that the more you will simply be that energy.

Natural characteristics of a woman in Woman Energy™:

* Women in Woman Energy™ live in the energy of ease and set the intention daily to be in this vibration and to be in the space of ease with every activity they begin.
* When a woman is in Woman Energy™ life feels hopeful and optimistic.
* She is centered, strong and empowered. She feels powerful inside.
* She knows what her needs and desires are and she is capable of meeting her needs and pursuing her desires.
* A woman in Woman Energy™ is present in her own life and she is fully engaged in it.
* A woman in Woman Energy™ is neither selfish nor does she allow others to be selfish.
* A woman in Woman Energy™ collaborates with others and does so with ease.

* She embodies the energy of joy, allowing, receiving and intuition.
* She feels safe in the world.
* This woman is authentic and magnetic to be around.
* Instead of giving to prove, she gifts everything. A woman in Woman Energy™ gifts her time, energy, attention, focus, talents and abilities. It is important to note that this doesn't mean she doesn't get paid for her employment. It simply means that she does everything with a gifting heart so that she is in a higher vibration.
* A woman in Woman Energy™ understands that having dreams and desires is an important part of the human experience and that pursuing these dreams and desires makes her a valuable example for other women to follow.
* Women in Woman Energy™ don't see themselves as victims. They see themselves as powerful, influential, purposeful and self-directed.
* A woman in Woman Energy™ is in an oxytocin state. She is calm and centered and her physiology supports this.
* A woman in Woman Energy™ is in an optimal balance of her feminine and masculine energies.
* A woman in Woman Energy™ has sufficient structure for her energy to flow optimally and she has sufficient flow for her life to move forward well.
* A woman in Woman Energy™ understands the importance of reprogramming her subconscious mind so that it supports the emotions she chooses to feel so that she can get out of and stay out of guilt.
* She also understands that there is no space in her life for guilt.
* She has nothing to prove so she doesn't require the approval of others.
* She believes she has the right to live her life on her terms.
* A woman in Woman Energy™ understands that stress is harming her and her family and she willingly establishes the boundaries she requires to significantly reduce her stress levels. In doing so, she is honoring herself.
* She understands the principle of pleasure and infuses pleasure into her daily life. Pleasure is a part of her way of being.
* She doesn't expect to do it all by herself. She understands that asking for support and assistance is not an act of weakness but an act of self-care and self- honoring.
* She understands that she can receive support without feeling obligated to give in return.
* A woman in this energy isn't a taker. She isn't taking from someone and she isn't expecting people to carry her so when she needs support and assistance, she is free to receive this and gifts support freely.

* A woman in Woman Energy™ establishes boundaries for her children, whether young or grown-up, because she knows that this is in their best interest and hers.
* Because she carries her own purse, a woman in Woman Energy™ doesn't take advantage of people. However, she has their backs in a way that doesn't leave her depleted.
* A woman in Woman Energy™ requires her husband/partner to be in Man Energy™ because all energy seeks balance.
* She believes that she does matter; that her needs matter; that taking care of her needs first is compassionate, not only to herself, but also to the others around her; and that she has the right to say no to anything and everything.
* A woman in Woman Energy™ lets her husband or partner know that if he doesn't do the task that he committed to doing, he is eroding her trust in him.
* A woman in Woman Energy™ doesn't waste endless hours on Facebook, Twitter, Instagram and the like.
* She understands that she needs to be very protective of her time, so she uses it to her best advantage.
* She feels a whole lot better about herself when she has interactions on social media with people who lift her up. She eliminates all interactions with people who drag her down.
* She has boundaries around when and with whom she responds on social media. She doesn't give everyone in the world access to her.
* She shuts off her electronic devices every evening.
* A woman in Woman Energy™ understands that to live a fulfilling life she is required to pursue her dreams and desires.
* Everything requires balance. Balance requires boundaries. A woman in Woman Energy™ understands this.
* A woman in Woman Energy™ understands that there is no healthy competition for women, except if they are in competitive sports, and that being and remaining in an oxytocin state is essential for her to move her dreams and desires forward.
* A woman in Woman Energy™ understands that she has a set amount of attention units each week.
* A woman in Woman Energy™, as best as she can, schedules important meetings and appointments for the beginning of the week and playtime at the end of the week.
* She understands that to move her dreams and desires forward, she must give them some attention units each week, even if the timing isn't right for them to be born now.
* She doesn't waste attention units with pointless worry.

* A woman in Woman Energy™ understands that the set amount of attention units gets used up easily through decision making. She allows and requires everyone in her life to make age-appropriate decisions.
* A woman in Woman Energy™ doesn't join committees that she has no interest in joining for she knows that these committees will take up attention units that would be better served in a different way.
* A woman in Woman Energy™ focuses on being grounded in her body so that her energy is not all up in her head being consumed with endless thinking and mind chatter.

To be grounded in her body, she focuses on bringing her energy out of her head and down into her belly, about four fingers below her belly button. By having energy in her lower belly and not up in her head, she is now able to be present and her life is not being run by her subconscious mind.

* A woman in Woman Energy™ understands that to thrive, she needs to release trapped emotions and negative subconscious programming.
* A woman in Woman Energy™ understands the importance of self-care and she makes it a priority.

Which of the characteristics listed do you naturally embody? List them here so that you can see them written down. This is empowering to actually see the ones that you naturally embody.

Which characteristics are not yet a part of your way of being? List them here. Do you have any resonance with each one?

Do these feel like they should be a part of who you are? If so, what thoughts, feelings, beliefs, subconscious programming or patterns stop you from embodying each one?

Why do the characteristics that are not yet a part of who you are and have no resonance with you feel that way to you?

Which characteristics don't connect with you in any way? List them here. Why do these feel unnatural to you?

Do these characteristics feel unattainable? Do they feel like ideals that are impossible to achieve? Would you want them to become a part of who you are?

What was your biggest awareness or ah-ha from this chapter?

Did you release the unsupportive thoughts, feelings, beliefs, subconscious programming or patterns that came up for you as you worked through this chapter? If not, why not? Don't cheat yourself by skipping this step.

Chapter 17

Changing Your Subconscious Programming

We have lots of energy blocking us from becoming Woman Energy™, our natural way of being. Our early life programming tells us this is how things are, no questions asked, and this is how things will be, no questions asked. As well, we have trapped emotions that are holding us back from making changes. If we want to become Woman Energy™ we need to release the thoughts, feelings, beliefs, subconscious programming and patterns that stop us from being that.

Key points in this chapter:

* All of your beliefs are someone else's beliefs and they become your "Because I said so" view of the world.
* Your original programming, whether good or bad, is the benchmark for all new information to be compared against.
* It is hard to change beliefs and patterns of behavior if they are different from what is programmed in you.
* Nothing that happens to us has meaning until we give it meaning. Unfortunately, the meanings we generally apply to our experiences are negative interpretations of ourselves based on our subconscious programming.
* Negative experiences are always "turned on" in our cells and create cellular memory. We have cellular memories on cells throughout our entire bodies and these cellular memories are always impacting us until they are released.

* Everything in the universe is energy. Your thoughts are energy. Your beliefs are energy. Your emotions are energy. Your body is made up of energy. Your cellular memories are energy. All energy vibrates and different things vibrate at different frequencies.

* If we feel a lot of lower vibrating emotions like jealousy, entitlement and apathy we are broadcasting out these vibrations. And, we will receive back these vibrations. So, we experience events that make us feel jealous, entitled, apathetic and the like.

* In addition to our original programming, incorrect meanings and charged cellular memories, we have emotions trapped in our bodies that constantly make it difficult for us to make changes.

* Emotions are just different chemicals that are released by our organs and glands. Our cells interpret these chemicals as particular emotions.

* The body is designed to process these chemicals fully and completely as we have different experiences.

* Not all emotions, or more accurately the chemicals that make up those emotions, are processed fully and we end up with trapped emotions.

* Trapped emotions can cause a lot of suffering, physically as well as mentally, emotionally and psychologically.

* To determine what emotions you have trapped, use Dr. Bradley Nelson's *The Emotion Code*™ book and *The Emotion Code Chart*™.

* When the human magnetic field is exposed to another magnetic field, surprising things happen. Trapped emotions can be released and negative thinking and programming can be changed.

* *Magnetic Field Release*™ will release the negative influences we have going on in our mind and body.

* Pay attention to all of the negative things you say about yourself. Pay attention to all of the negative programming that is directing your life.

* As you release these negative thoughts, feelings, beliefs, subconscious programming and patterns, what remains is your beautiful, brilliant self, which is connected to your highest self.

* You really are a brilliant diamond buried under negative programming.

* A woman in Woman Energy™ understands that to thrive, she needs to release both trapped emotions and negative subconscious programming. She understands that doing this work is part of her internal operating instructions.

When bad things happen to you, do you automatically believe it was because you deserved it or it was all your fault or some other negative meaning you have given to these experiences? If so, list these incorrect meanings.

What beliefs do you have about yourself that are undermining your self-esteem?

What negative things do you say to yourself?

In what areas of your life are you sabotaging yourself?

Are you open to changing your negative programming and releasing your trapped emotions? If yes, why? If not, why not?

Do you deserve to have greater happiness and more peace in your life? If not, why not?

Is it safe for you to be calmer and more peaceful? If not, why not?

Is it safe for you to be in control of your own life? If not, why not?

Do you deserve to feel more powerful? If not, why not?

Do you deserve to be present in your own life? If so, why? If not, why not?

Do you deserve to thrive? If so, why? If not, why not?

What was your biggest awareness or ah-ha from this chapter?

Did you release the unsupportive thoughts, feelings, beliefs, subconscious programming or patterns that came up for you as you worked through this chapter? If not, why not? Don't cheat yourself by skipping this step.

Section Five

Taking Care of Your Self

Chapter 18

✦ ✦ ✦

Is it Selfish to Take Care of Your Self?

Have you ever really stopped to think about what self-care means? As women, we somehow developed a definition of self-care that means it is all-consuming and either-or. This definition says that taking care of yourself requires all of your time, focus, energy and attention to the exclusion of everyone and everything or you don't give yourself any time and all of your time, focus, energy, and attention is given to everything and everyone but you. Neither of these extremes is healthy. Perhaps what you really need is a new definition of self-care that makes sense.

Key points in this chapter:

* We often struggle with the issue of taking care of ourselves.
* We have been conditioned to believe that every waking moment of every day needs to be committed to someone or something other than to ourselves.
* If you don't take care of yourself, you will become someone else's burden.
* If you really want to take care of your family, you will take care of yourself first.
* When women take care of themselves first, everyone in their family has the best opportunity to be healthy as well.
* When you don't take care of yourself, it can be truly devastating for both the physical and emotional health of the whole family.
* Taking care of yourself as a priority makes everyone in your family healthier.

* When adult females take better care of themselves, it tends to positively affect those around them, whoever they may be. This is true with your animal companions as well.
* Taking care of yourself is not a selfish act, but not taking care of yourself is. It is selfish to not take care of yourself. Not taking care of yourself has dramatic, negative impacts on your family.
* Taking care of yourself doesn't mean that you spend all day, every day tending to yourself at the expense of your job and everyone in your inner circle.
* Self-care means establishing healthy limits on what you do for others and having healthy expectations of what you require others to do for themselves.
* It means saying no to the activities that drain you and bring you no joy.
* Taking care of yourself also means that you need to do those things for yourself that you always expect others to do for you.
* Taking care of yourself means that you take some time for yourself to recharge your batteries.
* Self-care means investing your time in ways that enliven you.
* Time is your most precious resource. Time is finite.
* All other resources – energy, money, attention, focus - can be replenished and replaced.
* Be very, very protective of your time and invest it in ways that enrich your life.
* When you spend your time with people who don't matter, doing things that deplete you and having experiences that make you resentful and hostile, you aren't taking care of yourself.
* When you invest your time in people, activities and experiences that matter to you and lift you up, you are taking care of yourself.
* Only invest time and gift energy to people who feel you and your time matter. Having this boundary is a beautiful act of self-care.
* Going through your day holding your breath activates your fight or flight response. Holding your breath signals to your brain that you are in danger.
* Prolonged activation of your fight or flight response registers as stress in your body.
* Always, always, always remember to exhale.
* When you start to feel your fight or flight response activate, breathe in for four counts and breathe out for four counts. Do this four times. This will deactivate your fight or flight response. This is great self-care.
* A woman in Woman Energy™ understands the importance of self-care and she makes it a priority.

New Insight

As women, we get lost in the cycle of not taking care of ourselves because we are busy with everything and everyone else.

The **number one thing** your kids want and your spouse for that matter (unless he/she is a narcissist) is **for you to be healthy, happy and here.** When you aren't taking care of yourself and you let yourself get run down and sick, **your children believe it is all their fault.** I know I did. This is an enormous burden to place on your kids.

When kids see their mom go through some kind of illness that resulted from them not taking care of themselves, this experience changes the kids. Their world feels less safe. It takes away their freedom to engage fully in their own lives because there is a constant worry about the wellbeing of their mom.

If you do get sick and you don't take care of yourself, **your children believe they don't matter enough for you to take care of yourself and get well.** They believe that if they mattered more, you would want to be here.

Taking care of yourself is one of the **easiest ways** to **make your kids feel** safe, worthy and happy. Isn't that why you are doing everything that you are doing in the first place? I bet you never thought of it that way.

Take care of yourself today and every day and make your kids (and spouse) happy. It is a win-win for everybody.

Before reading The Thriving Woman's Guide to Setting Boundaries how did you feel about taking care of yourself? Do you have a different mindset regarding this now? If not, why not? Do you still believe it is selfish to take care of yourself? If so, what would it take for you to believe that taking care of yourself is self-full and necessary?

How did you feel when you read in the book that not taking care of yourself is self-ish?

What does self-care mean to you? Have you ever really thought about this? Are there specific things you do to take care of yourself? If so, list them. Do you do them daily?

Do you have healthy limits on what you do for others? What does this mean to you? How do you know when you have gone beyond these limits? If you don't have healthy limits, what is stopping you from having them? What thoughts, feelings, beliefs, subconscious programming or patterns prevent you from setting these limits?

Do you have healthy expectations of what you require others to do for themselves? What does this mean to you? Are you a bad person for expecting people to take age-appropriate action? Are you a better person for enabling others to be irresponsible for their lives?

Do you say no to activities that drain you and bring you no joy? What are these draining activities? What stops you from saying no? What thoughts, feelings, beliefs, subconscious programming or patterns prevent you from saying no to these activities?

Have you started to take care of for yourself those activities that you always expected others to take care of (especially if you are in Daughter Energy™)? What are these activities? Why did you expect others to take care of them for you? If you still expect others to take care of these, why? How does this serve you?

Do you take some time for yourself to recharge your batteries? What does this mean to you? If you don't take some time to recharge your batteries how does getting run down make you a better person?

Do you invest your time in ways that enliven you and enrich your life? In what ways do you do this? Do you give your time away in ways that deplete your life force? How and with whom? If you aren't investing your time and you are giving it away, why would you want to give away your most precious resource (time)?

Are you frivolous with your time? Do you spend your time with people who don't matter to you? If so, who are these people? Why do you spend your time with them? Do you spend your time with people who don't think you matter? Who are these people? Why do you spend time with people who don't think you matter?

How do you feel about only investing time and gifting energy to people who feel you and your time matter? Be honest here. Is this selfish or self-full? If it is selfish, how are you a better person for constantly giving your life force to takers?

Do you feel you have the right to limit or eliminate your interaction with the takers? If so, why? If not, why not?

Do you continue to do things that deplete you? Do you continuously have experiences that make you resentful and hostile? How do you really feel when you are doing/having these? Do these activities lift you up or drag you down? What are the activities that drag you down? What thoughts, feelings, beliefs subconscious programming or patterns stop you from saying no to these?

Does everything on your to-do list make you feel expanded or constricted? What makes you feel constricted? What would you like to drop from your list? What stops you from dropping it from your list? Who else can do it or how else can it be taken care of? Do you trust someone else to take care of it?

Are you holding your breath as you go through your day? Are you even aware that you are doing this? What stops you from exhaling?

Do you keep doing certain seasonal or "traditional" activities that hold no meaning for you? Do you do these activities from a giving heart or from a gifting heart? If these activities make you stressed and miserable, why do you keep doing them? Are you a better person for being stressed and miserable? How would you honestly feel if you stopped doing these? What stops you from saying no?

What was your biggest awareness or ah-ha from this chapter?

Did you release the unsupportive thoughts, feelings, beliefs, subconscious programming or patterns that came up for you as you worked through this chapter? If not, why not? Don't cheat yourself by skipping this step.

Chapter 19

✦ ✦ ✦

Powerful Ways to Take Care of Your Self

*T*he question of self-care really isn't whether it is selfish to take care of yourself but rather do you want to be healthy and vibrant? This is a matter of being responsible for your own well-being. No one else can be responsible for this. What if self-care is something that you simply incorporate into your day instead of it being some major event that you have to fit into your schedule? There are 62 self-care suggestions mentioned in *The Thriving Woman's Guide to Setting Boundaries*. Obviously, if you don't have children or if your children are grown, some of the suggestions don't apply to you. Most of the suggestions require mindfulness and not much more in terms of implementing them.

If you feel taking care of yourself is selfish, ask yourself, "How is it selfish to drink water throughout the day to keep yourself properly hydrated? How is it selfish to keep your legs uncrossed at your knees so that you aren't activating your stress response? How is it selfish to stop sucking in your gut so that your brain doesn't register a threat? How is it selfish to stop watching the news so that you aren't being bombarded by fear and bad news?" These are simple and powerful ways to enhance your well-being. They are easy to incorporate into your life. Each one adds to your wellness.

To this point perhaps it has simply been a matter of not having a useful definition of self-care or not having the right information to implement that has prevented you from taking care of yourself. Perhaps it is just an excuse for you to remain stuck and unhappy. The best place to start is to ask yourself what thoughts, feelings, beliefs, subconscious programming or patterns stop you from infusing these simple yet powerful suggestions into your life.

There are lots of powerful ways to take care of yourself. As you incorporate these into your day, you will be building up your health and well-being.

Key points in the chapter:

* The most important act of self-care is to stop saying that you don't deserve some time to yourself.
* Physical self-care includes anything to do with your physical body and your physical environment.
* Mental self-care includes anything to do with your mind and your thought processes. These include conscious and subconscious activities including intention, thinking, creativeness, worrying and doubt.
* Emotional self-care includes anything to do with your emotions and lessening your emotional reaction to life's events.
* Psychological self-care is about bringing congruence to the conscious mind and the subconscious mind and behaving in ways that allow for that.
* Psychic self-care attends to the extrasensory and extraordinary aspects of non-physical and non-mental perception.
* Our spirit is the life force that animates our physical body. Spiritual self-care helps us connect to our spirit which is important for our overall health and well-being.
* Some things that you can do to take care of yourself cross categories.

Do you really want to take care of yourself? If so, why? If not, why not? If not, are you stuck in martyrdom? If you are, how is this working for you? What thoughts, feelings, beliefs, subconscious programming or patterns keep you stuck in this energy? Do you have the right to let these go so that you can take care of yourself? If not, who says so?

Does self-care feel difficult to do? Is it difficult because you have never really thought about what it means? Is it difficult because you haven't had the information you required to take right action?

Which self-care suggestions resonated with you as you read them? Have you infused these into your life? If not, why not?

Which self-care suggestions would you like to infuse into your life? What stops you from infusing them into your life? As you write these down has it occurred to you that you need to change your schedule to honor yourself more? Are you willing to do that?

Which self-care suggestions seem impossible for you to infuse into your life? Why?

How would you really feel if you took proper care of yourself?

What was your biggest awareness or ah-ha from this chapter?

Did you release the unsupportive thoughts, feelings, beliefs, subconscious program-ming or patterns that came up for you as you worked through this chapter? If not, why not? Don't cheat yourself by skipping this step

Additional Titles in The Thriving Woman's Guide to™ series

The Thriving Woman's Guide to Setting Boundaries

Kim Buck, M.B.A.

*B*eing the dependable one drains you of your life force, your dreams and any sense of sanity. My wish for you is that you understand from my story that your story doesn't have to go this way. If you are starting on this path, know to your core that you can say no. Know to your core that you have the right to set boundaries and live your life in a more peaceful, engaged way. Know to your core that you are not here, on earth, to save everyone. That is not your job. That is not your responsibility. Know to your core that you deserve to live your life and not carry others through theirs.

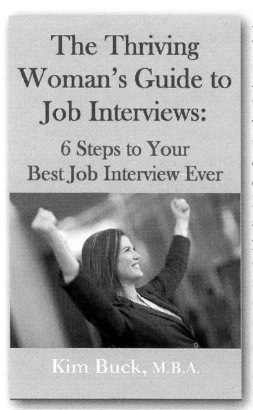

The Thriving Woman's Guide to Job Interviews:

6 Steps to Your Best Job Interview Ever

Kim Buck, M.B.A.

Most of what happens in an interview is based on the steps women take before they get to the interview. In Section One, Before the Interview, in *The Thriving Woman's Guide to Job Interviews: 6 Steps to Your Best Job Interview Ever,* women are taught how to research the company they are interviewing with so they know how they would add value there. The section also covers all of the elements of appearance, including clothing, jewelry, hair, makeup and fragrance. It shows women how to identify their strengths and weaknesses in a way that helps women have a greater sense of themselves. This section also guides women on how to answer the question, "What do you see yourself doing in 5 years?" so that women clearly understand where they are in their careers and what it will take for them to move forward. Section Two, The Interview, covers all components of an interview including the importance of being on time, how to sit, what to do with your phone and how to breathe. Section Three, After the Interview, explains the simple follow-up process and Section Four, Simple Energy Tips, shares powerful processes women can do before the interview to feel less stressed and more focused.

48747406R00123

Made in the USA
Charleston, SC
07 November 2015